GW01255235

General notes to the teacher

These copymasters are designed to help children undertake some of the mapping exercises in *Going Places: Mapping Skills*. In addition, suggestions are given for using the maps for other mapping activities. It is, however, important to see mapping activities in context. The following points should be considered.

1. Children's own perceptions of maps

Children should be encouraged to draw maps from memory – mental maps. These maps will be unique to individual children, expressing their own particular perceptions of the world. The 'marking' of such maps should be undertaken, if at all, with great sensitivity. It is often interesting to look at the wide range of different types of maps drawn from memory by children in response to the same instruction, e.g. "Draw a map of your bedroom." Allowing children to draw maps of their favourite stories or rhymes will also give them valuable confidence.

2. Children's experiences

Many of the mapping exercises contained in this book can be applied to different parts of the environment with which junior school children are familiar, such as the classroom, school and school grounds. All the children in a class share similar experiences of these places. With other environments, such as the home, street and neighbourhood, each child's experience tends to be unique. It is obviously useful to have maps of the school, school grounds and neighbourhood available for use with pupils. Maps can also be used to broaden a child's experience.

3. The content, ideas, skills and attitudes underpinning geography, environmental studies and thematic work

Mapping skills are skills which it is necessary for pupils to develop in order to understand the world around them. A full range of these skills is developed in *Going Places: Mapping Skills*. Other skills which can be practised from maps and map data such as observation, collecting, recording and classifying information are built into some of the exercises. Work related to key ideas such as distribution, pattern, relationship, movement, area and region can also be planned with the maps in these copymasters.

4. Maps are models

All maps are simplifications of the real world. They are, in effect, models. In order to represent elements of the real world, symbols are used and some things are missed off the map. Children need to use their skills and understanding in order to read and decode maps.

All maps consist of dots, lines and/or patches. They may or may not contain words. Hence, an ability to describe the distribution of such dots, lines and patches, the patterns they show, the way they interrelate and the movements which may result from these distributions is fundamental to an understanding of maps.

5. Mapping vocabulary

There are particular words which are used regularly when dealing with maps. It is important for children to know the meaning of these special words and their importance when using maps. Key mapping words have been picked out in bold print or in the headings in *Going Places: Mapping Skills*. The ability to use these words correctly and in context whenever possible will help children with their understanding of maps.

6. Maps as resources and tools

Maps are one of the resources which we use regularly in everyday life to help us develop our understanding and increase our awareness. It is a useful activity with junior school children to collect examples of the sorts of maps they may come into contact with in everyday life. These could then be made into an interesting classroom or corridor display.

The copymaster activities that follow should give you ample opportunity to select appropriate ones for your class. You may wish to devise further activities of your own along these lines.

Thomas Nelson and Sons Ltd
Nelson House   Mayfield Road
Walton-on-Thames   Surrey
KT12 5PL   UK

51 York Place
Edinburgh
EH1 3JD   UK

Thomas Nelson (Hong Kong) Ltd
Toppan Building 10/F
22A Westlands Road
Quarry Bay   Hong Kong

Distributed in Australia by

Thomas Nelson Australia
480 La Trobe Street
Melbourne   Victoria 3000
and in Sydney, Brisbane, Adelaide and Perth

© Malcolm Renwick and Bill Pick 1987

First published by Thomas Nelson & Sons Ltd 1987

ISBN 0-17-425441-5
Print No. 01

Printed in UK

Copymaster activities

Copymaster 1

1. Answer the questions in *Going Places: Mapping Skills.*
2. a. Which two objects have a rectangular or oblong shape?
   b. Which two objects have a circular shape?
   c. Which object is shaped like a hexagon (i.e. with six sides)?
3. Describe in words the plan view of   a. the fork   b. the cake   c. the teapot
4. For each of the following, draw a set of plan views: a. three toys   b. three pieces of dining room furniture   c. three things in the garden   d. three things in the bathroom

Copymaster 2

1. Answer the questions in *Going Places: Mapping Skills.*
2. You have just come into the main entrance of the school. Match up each of the directions below with the appropriate place:
   1. First door on the left.   a. Kitchen
   2. Straight ahead.   b. Hall
   3. Turn left, first door on the   c. Garden
      right.
   4. Turn left. It's at the end of   d. Girls' toilet
      the main corridor.
   5. Left down the corridor.   e. Secretary's office
      Fourth door on the left.
3. The door into the garden from the corridor is blocked. A visitor is in the entrance. Describe two other ways she could get to the animal corner.
4. You have just come through the main entrance. Do you have to go left, right or straight on to get to   a. the hall   b. the toilets   c. the secretary's office   d. the kitchen?
5. What shape is   a. the hall   b. the secretary's office   c. the secretary's office and the head's room together?
6. Read this carefully, then answer the questions:
   Jane arrives at school by the front entrance. She goes to the toilet then to her class. It is the one near the door to the garden. She goes to the hall for assembly then back to class. She takes a message to the headteacher and one to Mrs Mardia, who teaches in the class next to the girls' toilets. Jane goes back to class then out to play. After play she goes back to her class. Then it is her turn to clean out the animals. At lunchtime she goes to wash her hands and then to the hall for her lunch. Afterwards she goes out to play.
   Solomon also arrives at school and goes in at the main entrance. He is in Mrs Mardia's class. He goes straight there. The class goes to assembly. After assembly he wants to go to the toilet. Before that he has to take a message to the kitchen. Then he goes back to class. He goes out to play at playtime then back to class. At lunchtime he too goes to the hall before going out to play.
   a. Draw a blue line showing Jane's movements around school that morning.
   b. Draw a red line showing Solomon's movements.
   c. Which parts of the school do these two pupils use most?
7. Make a land use map of the school by colouring these different uses in different colours. Make a key.
   a. Areas used by a class
   b. Areas used for moving about (corridors or routeways)
   c. Areas used by the whole school
   d. Area for food preparation
   e. Area used for administration
   f. Areas used for play

Copymaster 3

1. Answer the questions in *Going Places: Mapping Skills.*
2. Arrange the furniture as you would like it.
3. Imagine that a friend is coming to stay. You are going to put a mattress on the living room floor. Where would you put it? How would you re-arrange the furniture?
4. A friend comes with a baby in a pram. The pram must not go near the doors or the baby may be in a draught. It must not be too near the fire either. Where would you put it? Re-arrange the rest of the furniture.
5. The sentences below describe Karl's evening. Read them and then draw his movements about the living room.
   He comes in and switches the fire on. He flops in a chair. Getting up quickly, he switches the TV on. He goes to the kitchen for a drink, comes back, sits down and watches TV. He helps his mum lay the table and then sits down for his tea. As well as watching TV afterwards he sits with his mum at the table to play a game. He then goes to help with the washing up.

Copymaster 4

1. Using grid reference numbers, describe the teacher's route as she goes round the class to look at the children's work.
2. If the teacher is facing north when sitting at her desk, what direction is: a. the door from her   b. Kevin from Jenny   c. Jenny from Inderpal   d. Inderpal from the door?
3. How many groups are there of   a. two children   b. three children   c. four children   d. five children?
   e. How many children are on their own?
4. Arrange the named children in order of their distance from the door. Put the nearest first, the furthest away last.
5. Do the same for the distance of each child from the teacher.
6. Fill in the blank spaces in these sentences.
   a. This is a _____ of a classroom.   (plan, picture)
   b. It shows the shape of the desks, chairs, cupboards as seen directly from _____.   (above, below, anywhere)
   c. The blackboard is between the door and _____.   (the teacher, Inderpal, Jenny, Kevin)
   d. The door is _____ Inderpal.   (behind, in front of, to the right of)
   e. Jenny sits to the _____ of Kevin.   (left, right)

Side view   **Top view**   **Plan**

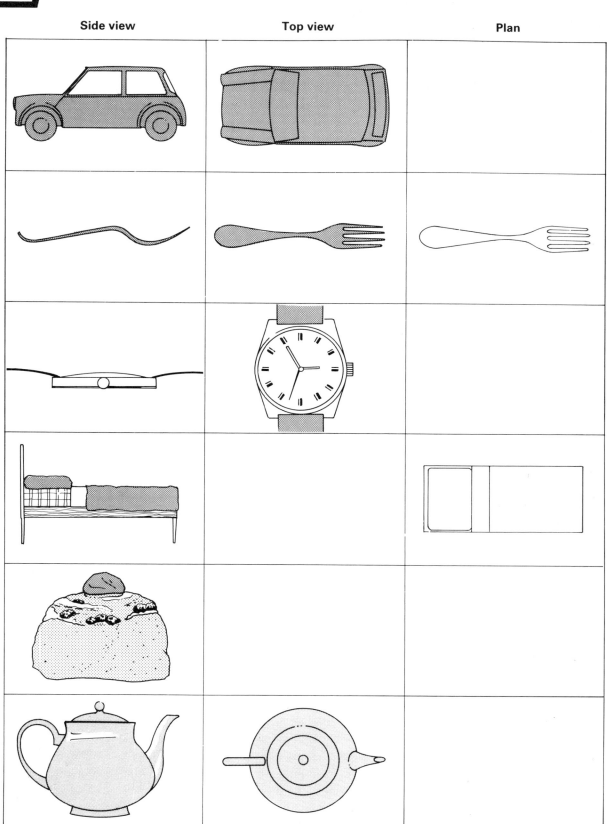

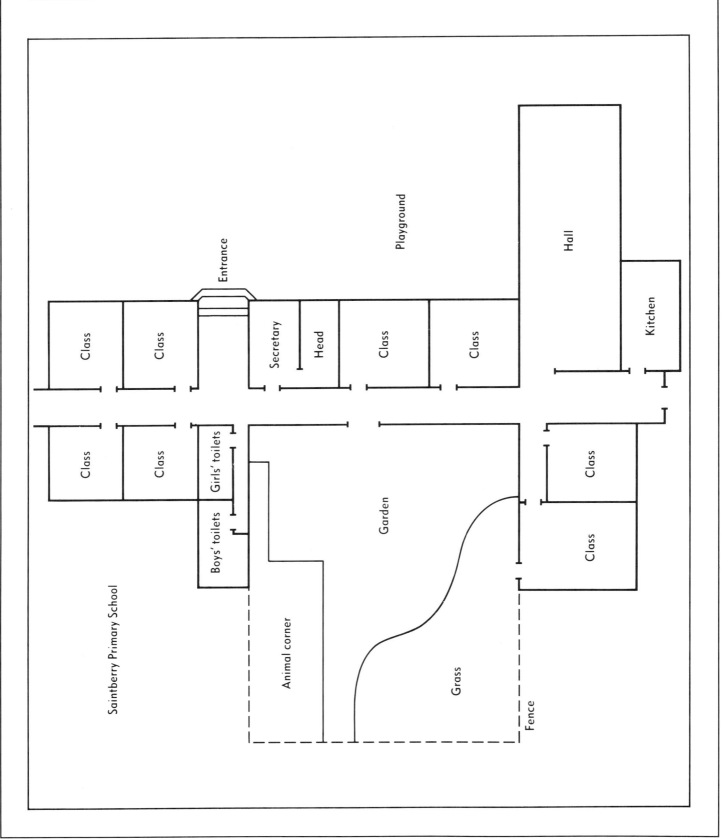

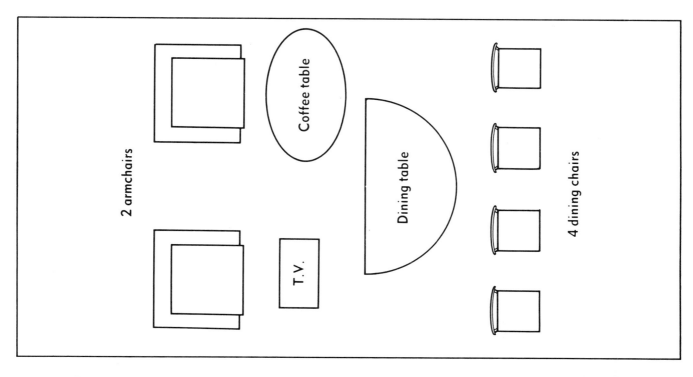

2 armchairs

Coffee table

Dining table

4 dining chairs

T.V.

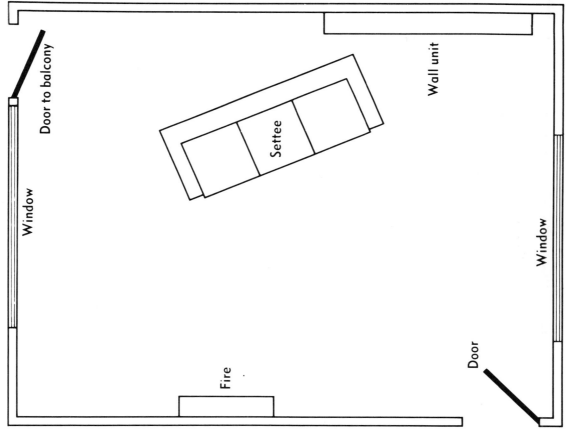

Door to balcony

Window

Settee

Wall unit

Window

Fire

Door

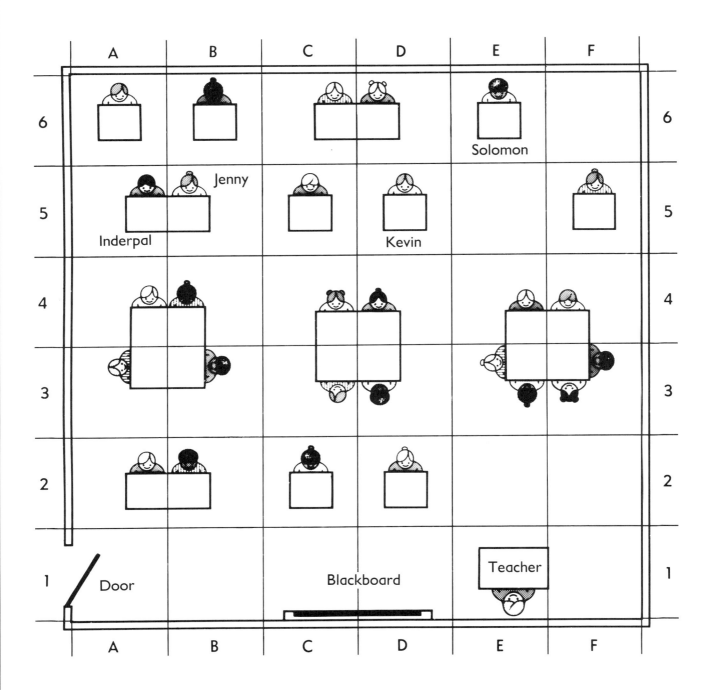

5 Map of the British Isles

Scotland
Inverness
Aberdeen
Dundee
Perth
Stirling
Edinburgh
Glasgow
Kilmarnock
Ayr
Dumfries
Londonderry
Northern Ireland
Belfast
Carlisle
Newcastle upon Tyne
Sunderland
Workington
Middlesbrough
York
Blackpool
Bradford
Leeds
Kingston upon Hull
Huddersfield
Galway
Republic of Ireland
Dublin
Liverpool
Manchester
Sheffield
Stoke on Trent
Derby
Nottingham
Limerick
Wolverhampton
Walsall
Leicester
Norwich
Waterford
Birmingham
Coventry
Cambridge
Northampton
Cork
Wales
England
Ipswich
Luton
Newport
Oxford
Southend
Swansea
Bristol
Cardiff
Reading
London
Dover
Taunton
Southampton
Brighton
Exeter
Bournemouth
Portsmouth
Plymouth
Torbay
Country boundary
Very large built-up areas
Main towns
Scale 1:4.5 million
0 45 90 135 180
kilometres

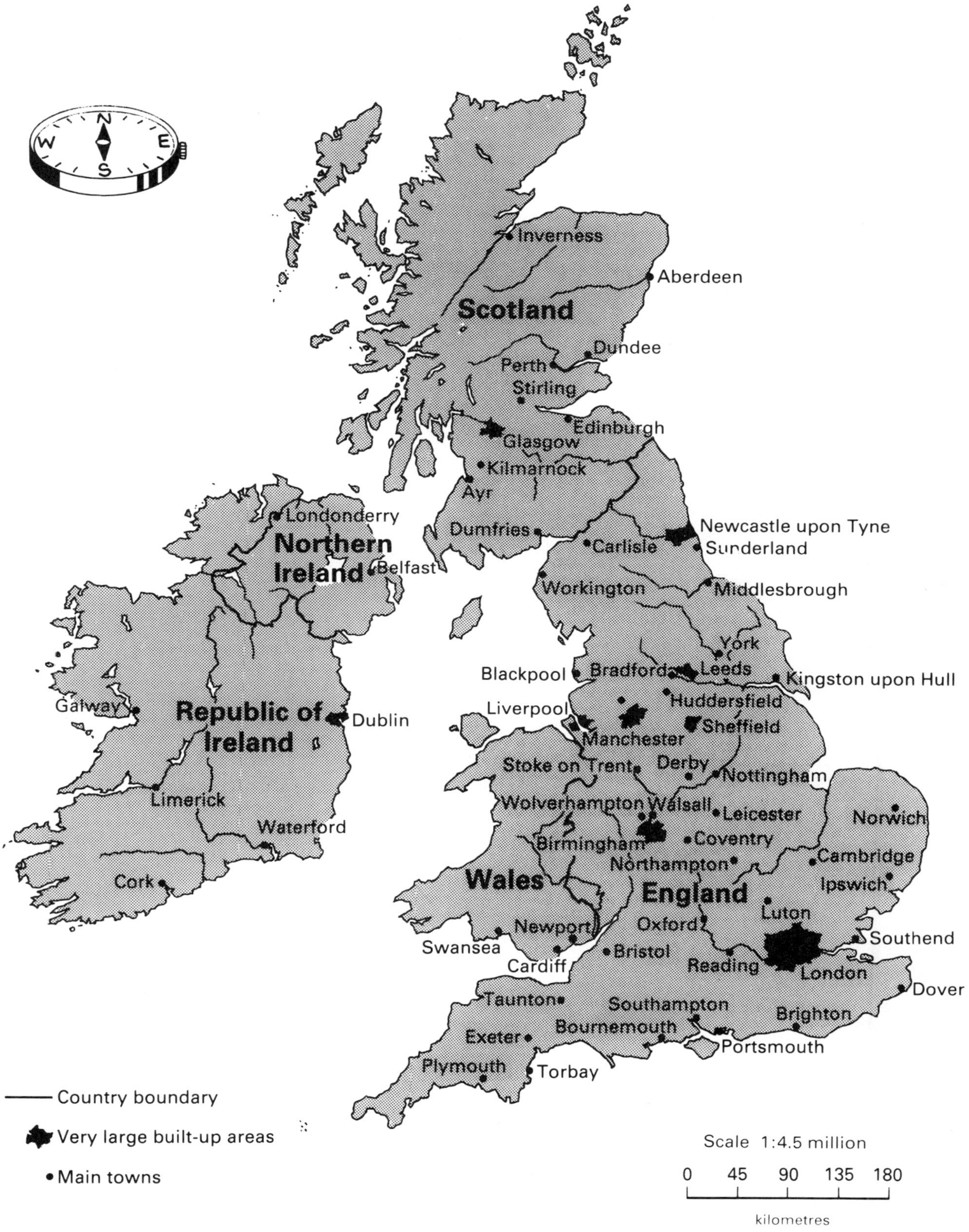

6 Map of Europe

Scale 1:19 million

0   190   380   570   760

kilometres

—— Country boundary

■ Capital town

● Other important town

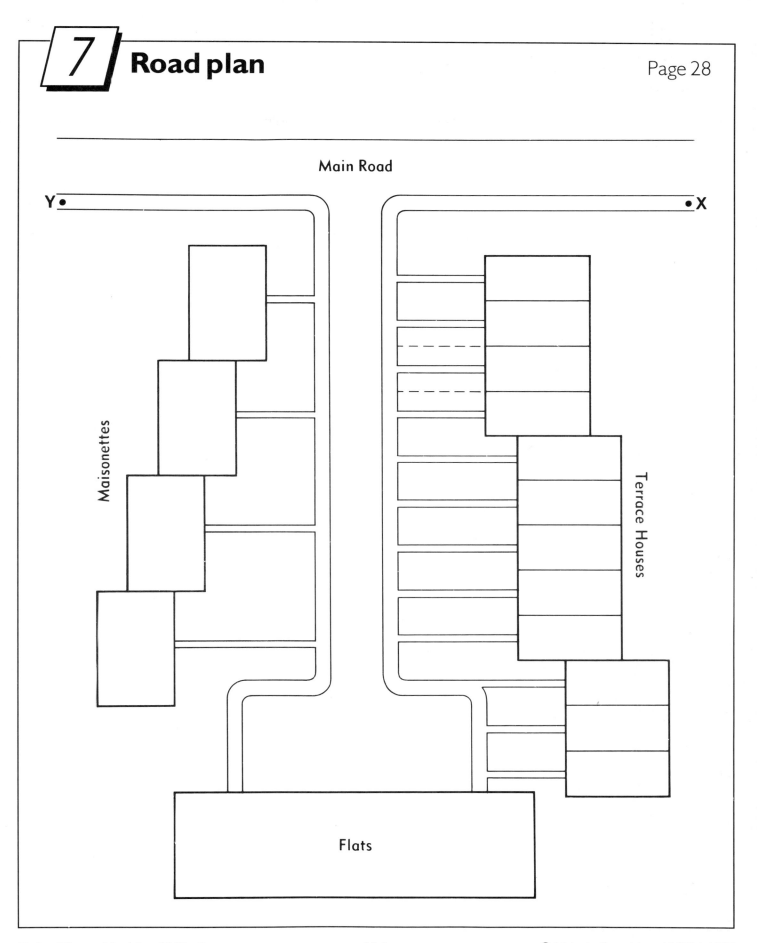

Main Road

Y•

•X

Maisonettes

Terrace Houses

Flats

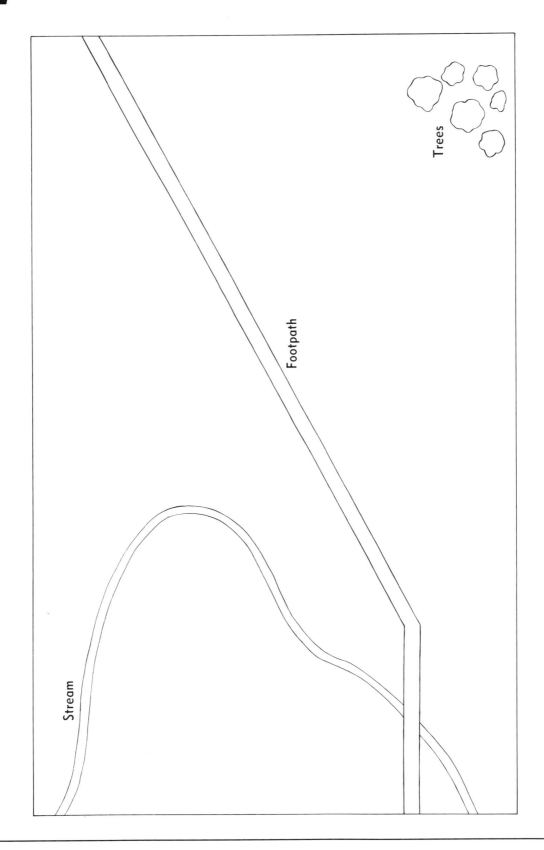

Trees

Footpath

Stream

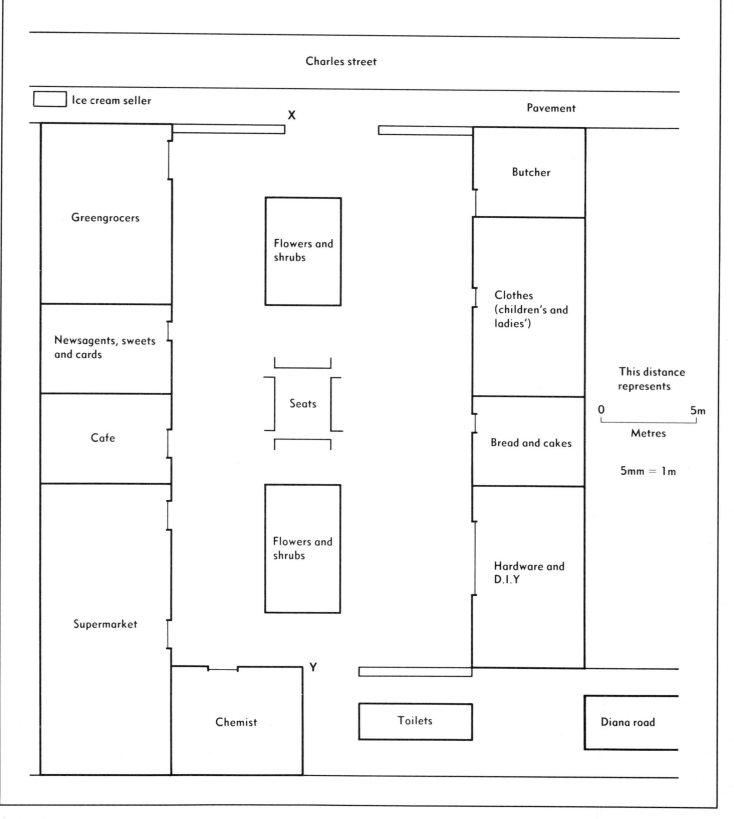

Charles street

Ice cream seller

Pavement

X

Butcher

Greengrocers

Flowers and shrubs

Clothes (children's and ladies')

Newsagents, sweets and cards

This distance represents

0   5m

Metres

Seats

5mm = 1m

Cafe

Bread and cakes

Flowers and shrubs

Hardware and D.I.Y

Supermarket

Y

Chemist

Toilets

Diana road

10 Beach plan

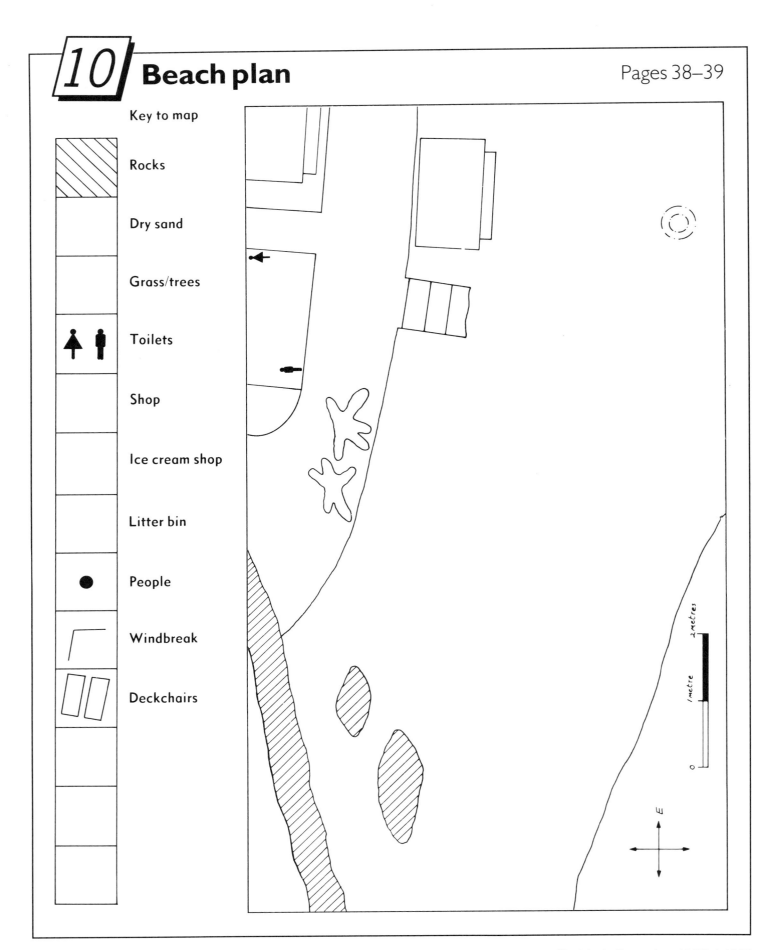

Key to map

Rocks

Dry sand

Grass/trees

Toilets

Shop

Ice cream shop

Litter bin

People

Windbreak

Deckchairs

Neighbourhood map

Pages 40, 41, 42

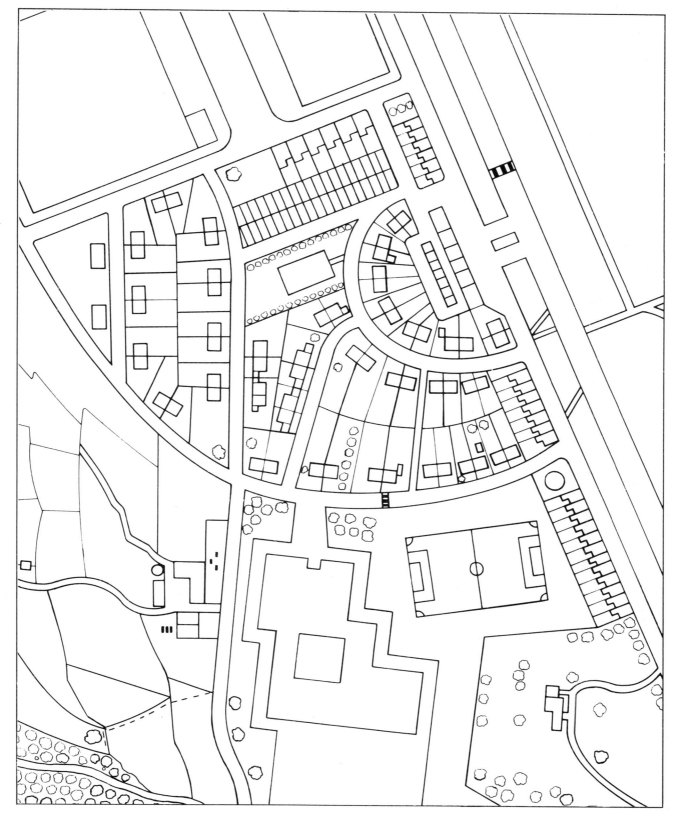

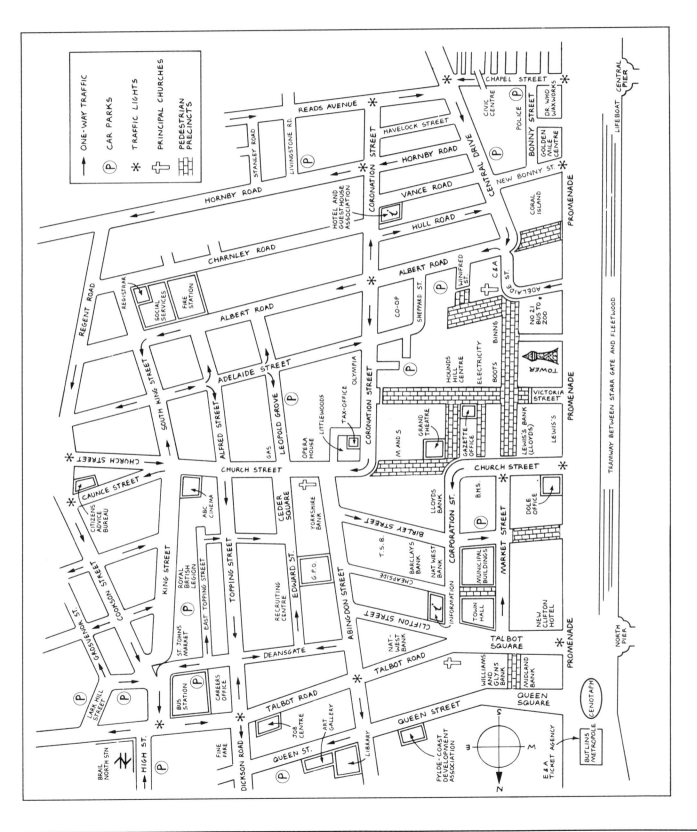

Copymaster 5

1. Name each of the five countries shown.
2. Name two towns in each of the five countries.
3. Which country lies: a. north of England b. south-west of Scotland c. north of the Republic of Ireland d. east of Wales e. east of the Republic of Ireland?
4. Which country covers the largest area?
5. Which is nearer to
   a. Oxford   — Cambridge or Dover?
   b. Edinburgh   — Dundee or Kilmarnock?
   c. Cardiff   — Swansea or Newport?
6. Arrange these towns in order of nearness to London: Bournemouth, Plymouth, Taunton, Torbay, Bristol.
7. How far is it from Derby to a. Leeds b. Norwich c. Bristol?
8. In which direction would you be going if you were travelling from:
   a. Waterford to Londonderry?
   b. Leeds to Derby?
   c. Newcastle to Carlisle?
   d. Inverness to Aberdeen?

Copymaster 6

Look at the map on page 27 of *Going Places: Mapping Skills*. Then use your copymaster to answer the questions below.

1. Mark with a red dot each capital town which is on a coast.
2. Mark with a brown dot each capital town inland.
3. Which capital is furthest from the sea?
4. Find out which countries are in the E.E.C. Colour them in yellow.
5. What is the name of: a. the smallest country on the map b. the country shaped like a leg c. two countries which have one coast on the Mediterranean and one on the Atlantic?
6. In which direction would you travel if you flew from:
   a. Rome to Munich?
   b. Munich to Budapest?
   c. Belgrade to Lyon?
   d. Bonn to Berne?
   e. London to Kiev?
   f. Dublin to Hamburg?
7. For each of these flights, fill in this table. The first one is done for you.

	From	Over	To
Rome to Munich	Italy	Austria	W. Germany
Munich to Budapest			
Belgrade to Lyon			
Bonn to Berne			
London to Kiev			
Dublin to Hamburg			

Copymaster 7

1. Colour the living areas red, the garden areas green, the roads and footpaths yellow. Describe the patterns shown.
2. Draw the postman's route on the map.
3. Three boys want to play cricket in the street. Mark with a **c** where they should play.
4. Four girls also want to play outside with their ball. Mark with a **b** where they could play.
5. Do either the boys or the girls interfere with the postman's route?
6. As the postman walks from Main Road to the flats, what would be a. on his left b. on his right?
   How many paths to houses would he pass on his left?

Copymaster 8

1. Answer the questions in *Going Places: Mapping Skills*.
2. Shade in different colours:
   a. the area between the stream and the footpath
   b. the area below the footpath
   c. the area to the left of the stream
3. One of these areas is for flowers, paths and seats. One is for young children to play. There will be swings and other playthings. One area will be for ball games.
   Say which area will be used for each of these things. Then say why you have chosen it.
   Now plan where the seats, paths, flower beds and litter bins will go. Draw them on your plan.
4. Decide what playthings you want in the play area. Arrange them on the plan too. Use symbols.
5. Do you think it a good or bad idea to have these three areas kept separate? Give your reasons.
6. Read this description of how the park used to be. On another copymaster, mark where you think each of the things may have been.
   There were big gates at the entrance to the park. Along the path there were five seats with flower troughs between them. There was a round bandstand near the trees with a drinking fountain nearby. Part of the stream had been widened to make a small boating lake. There was a small park keeper's hut close to the footpath. One litter bin was found near each end of the path.

Copymaster 9

1. Answer the questions in *Going Places: Mapping Skills*.
2. Colour the map. Colour the footpaths and roads yellow, and the food shops blue.
3. Describe the pattern of a. the footpaths b. the food shops
4. How far is it from X to Y a. in a straight line b. avoiding the flower beds?
5. How far is it from the seats to a. the toilet b. the chemist c. the butcher?
6. Make up your own shopping list. Draw your route on the map.
7. Mark where you think the busiest places and the quietest places are likely to be.
8. Can you find a better place for the ice cream seller to stand? Say why you think your place is better.

Copymaster 10

1. Answer the questions in *Going Places: Mapping Skills*.
2. Complete each of these sentences by putting in the correct compass direction.
   a. The shop is in the _____ corner of the map.
   b. The sea is in the _____ corner of the map.
   c. The sandcastle is in the _____ corner of the map.
   d. The lady sunbathing walks to the _____ to get an ice cream.
   e. The man near the steps walks _____ to get to the sea or _____ to get to the toilets.
   f. The road runs from _____ to _____ .
3. Mark these on the map:
   a. two people buying candyfloss
   b. someone standing near the trees
   c. a family of four close to the rocks
   d. a litter bin between the steps and the ice cream kiosk
   e. five children running along the wet sand
4. The wind changes direction. It starts to blow from the north-east. Show where you now put the windbreak.
5. How far would this family have to go:
   a. to get an ice cream?
   b. to get into the sea?
   c. to the toilets?

Copymaster 11

Use this map and the picture on page 43.

1. Answer the questions in *Going Places: Mapping Skills*.
2. On your copymaster, name:
   the school, the church, the football field, the farm, a terrace of houses, a semi-detached house, a row of garages, a stream, the factory, the large detached house.
3. Draw these routes on the map:
   a. the farmer as he goes to church
   b. from the school to the factory for a visit
   c. from the detached house to the shops
   d. delivering leaflets to every house in the area
   e. the building worker's route to the shops
4. Choose 6 houses. Put a child's name by each one. Now draw the routes of each of the children to the playground near the main road. Remember to use the zebra crossing. Who has the shortest route? Who has the longest route?
5. Look for different road junctions.
   a. Mark with a **T** five ⊤⊢ junctions.
   b. Mark with a **C** one ⊣⊢ crossroad junction.
   c. Mark with a **Y** one junction where the roads meet at an angle.
6. Design a layout for the inner garden at the school. Show it as a plan.
7. Choose three good places for a post box. Which is the best place?

Copymaster 12

1. If you were walking from the Dr. Who Waxworks along the Promenade to the New Clifton Hotel:
   a. In which direction would you be going?
   b. How many sets of traffic lights would you pass?
   c. Name three streets you would have to cross.
2. Describe how you would go on foot from the Golden Mile Centre to   a. Boots   b. The Fire Station. Draw your routes on the map.
3. Which of the two places in Question 2 could you go to in a car? Say why you could not go to the other one in a car.
4. Follow these directions and draw this route on your map.
   From outside the Grand Theatre walk south along the pedestrian precinct. Turn east to Coronation Street. Turn south along Coronation Street to the second crossroads. Turn left (east).
   Which road are you now walking along?
5. In which direction is the traffic moving along these one-way streets:
   a. Coronation Street
   b. Market Street
   c. Albert Road
   d. Adelaide Street?
6. Complete these sentences by choosing the correct direction from this list: NE, SW, NW, SE.
   a. The British Rail North Station is in the _____ corner of the map.
   b. The Dr. Who Waxworks is in the _____ corner of the map.
   c. The Butlins Metropole is in the _____ corner of the map.
7. Finish off these directions. The person is at Lewis's and wants to get to the Bus Station.
   Go along Church Street and into Corporation Street. Then go past the Information Office . . .
8. Now direct someone from the Opera House to the Golden Mile Centre.
9. Use the map key provided. How many of these can you find:
   a. information centres   b. car parks   c. churches?